سیری در آثار هنری اسلامی

Journey through Islamic Art

Na'ima bint Robert & Diana Mayo

Touch the arrow with TalkingPEN to start

Start   Info   English   Language

MANTRA
LINGUA

من داستانهای زیادی در باره شهرهای سمرقند و بغداد،
مغولها در هند و اعراب مراکشی در اسپانیا شنیده ام.

I heard tales about the cities of Samarkand and Baghdad,
About the Moghuls in India and the Moors in Spain.

من رشته های ابریشمی تاریخ را به دستم بستم و با
آنها افکارم به ساعت زمان پیوست. ساعت زمانی که مرا
به یک سفر شگفت انگیز برد.سیاحتی در آثار هنری اسلامی.

I gathered silken threads of history in my hands and,
With them, my mind wove a flying cloak:
A cloak that took me on an amazing voyage
Through the art of the Islamic world.

ساعت زمان مرا به شهر قدیمی بغداد برد.
منزلگاه مسجد ها، حمّامهای عمومی،
خط سیر مسابقه ها و جایگاههای تماشاچیان.

My cloak took me to the old city of Baghdad,
Home to mosques, public baths,
racetracks, and pavilions.

شهر قلعه های محکم صحرایی که دیوارهای آنها
با نقاشیهایی از سقف تا زمین مزیّن شده است.
منزلگاه سامره بزرگترین مسجد دنیا که بنظر میرسد
نماز گزاران را روی ابرها میخواند.

Home to fortified desert castles,
Adorned with wall-paintings from floor to ceiling.
The largest mosque in the world called Samarra its home,
I imagined that the call to prayer reached me in the clouds.

ساعت زمان مرا به سوی مسلمانان اسپانیا می برد
جایی که شرق به غرب می پیوندد.
از برابر دانشمندان، کاشفان،
و ستاره شناسان دربار که محدوده دانش بشری
را ارزیابی میکنند عبور می کنم.

My cloak took me to Muslim Spain,
Where the East met the West.
I passed scientists, inventors and court astronomers,
Testing the limits of human knowledge.

اینجا به یک باغچه تزیینی میرسم.
از فوارها وباغی عطرآگین عبور می کنم.

There, I wandered through ornamental courtyards,
Past fountains and scented gardens.

میراث هنری اسلام و اسپانیا
بهم آمیخته است.
قصر ال حمرا و مسجد بزرگ
گردبا را عرضه کرده است.
گنبدها، موزاییک ها
و گذرگاههای طاقدار
چشمان مشتاق مرا
خیره کرده است.

The artistic heritage
of Islam and Spain
Fused to create the
Al Hambra palace
and the great mosque
of Cordoba.
Domes, mosaics and
archways greeted my
eager eyes.

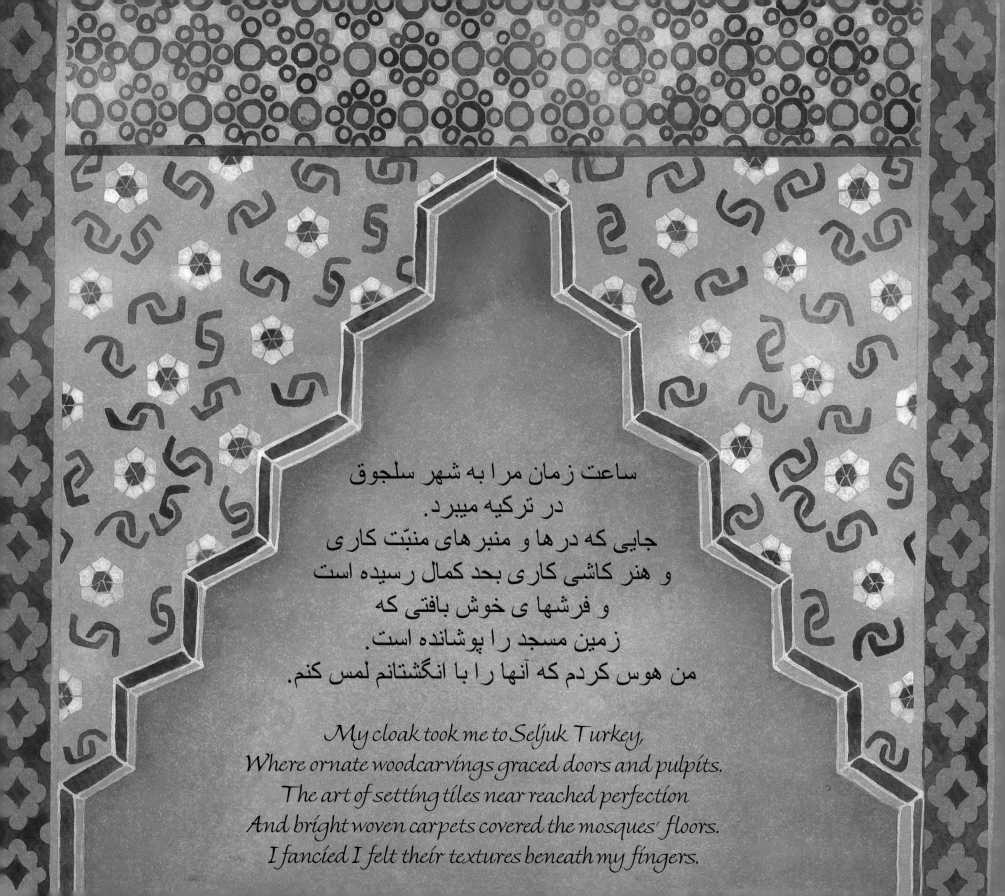

ساعت زمان مرا به شهر سلجوق
در ترکیه میبرد.
جایی که درها و منبرهای منبّت کاری
و هنر کاشی کاری بحد کمال رسیده است
و فرشها ی خوش بافتی که
زمین مسجد را پوشانده است.
من هوس کردم که آنها را با انگشتانم لمس کنم.

My cloak took me to Seljuk Turkey,
Where ornate woodcarvings graced doors and pulpits.
The art of setting tiles near reached perfection
And bright woven carpets covered the mosques' floors.
I fancied I felt their textures beneath my fingers.

ساعت زمان مرا به
سمرقند شهر تیمور لنگ برد.
جایی که همه صنعتگران دنیا جمع شده بودند.

My cloak took me to the Samarkand
of Timur 'the Lame'
Where artisans from around the
world were gathered.

سنگ تراشان از هند.
خطاطان از ایران.

Stonemasons from India,
calligraphers from Persia,

نقره کاران از ترکیه
و ابریشم بافان از دمشق.

Silversmiths from Turkey and
silk-weavers from Damascus.

همه را برای جاودانگی شهرش به اسارت گرفته بود.
در حالیکه قصر او چادرش بود، خانه بدوشی در برش بود.

All brought back as captives, to beautify his city,
While his palace was a tent – a nomad to the end.

ساعت زمان مرا به خیابانهای اگرا برد،
جایی که شهرت تاج محل بازار را به همهمه آورده بود.

My cloak took me to the streets of Agra,
Where rumours of the Taj Mahal filled buzzing bazaars.

بنایی که از پیمانی در بستر مرگ ساخته شده است،
با جامه ایی از مرمر سفید
در نور سوسو میزند.

A building born from a deathbed promise,
Its garment of white marble
Shimmered in the light.

المشرق

کتیبه های خطی اقتباس شده از قرآن،
کاشی کاری های گلدار سبک اسلامی و
طرحهای هندسی با هم هم آهنگی خاصی دارند،
و شعری که آنرا "پگاه روشن" نامیدند.
ایکاش زیبایی آن نمایانگر زندگی باشد
نه اینکه پنهان کننده مرگ.

صباح الفجر

Calligraphic inscriptions from the Qur'aan,
Floral arabesques and geometric designs
all harmonised
And the poets named her 'Dawn's bright face'.
I wished its beauty could grace the living
and not enshroud the dead.

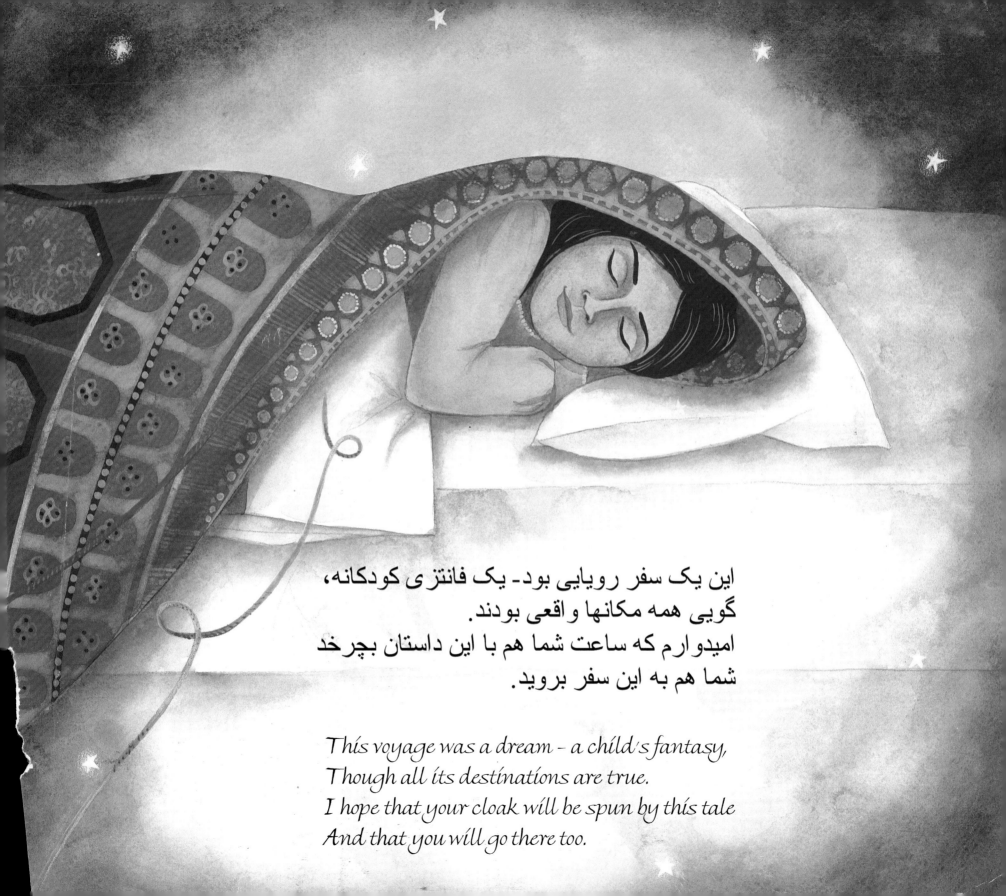

این یک سفر رویایی بود- یک فانتزی کودکانه،
گویی همه مکانها واقعی بودند.
امیدوارم که ساعت شما هم با این داستان بچرخد
شما هم به این سفر بروید.

This voyage was a dream - a child's fantasy,
Though all its destinations are true.
I hope that your cloak will be spun by this tale
And that you will go there too.

Here are some explanations to help you enjoy the story:

Samarra
In the 9th century, after the foundation of Baghdad, the Caliph (ruler) moved his capital to the splendid city of Samarra. The Great Mosque was once the largest mosque in the Islamic world and rises to a height of 52 meters.

Islamic Spain was established in the 8th century by Muslims from North Africa who were known as Moors. For over three hundred years, Muslims, Christians and Jews lived together in a Golden Age when learning, art and culture flourished.

Seljuk Turkey was one of the eras in Islamic history. The Seljuks were Muslim rulers who took control of Persia and Turkey. Seljuk Turkey became the centre of excellence in weaving, ceramic painting and wood carving.

Born in the 14th century, **Timur 'the Lame'**, also known as Tamerlane, was a fierce and determined Mongol warrior who loved art. Whenever his armies invaded foreign cities, he would take care to protect the artisans and take them back to beautify his city, Samarkand.

The **Taj Mahal** was a monument built by the Mughal Emperor Shah Jahan in 1631 as a tribute to his loving wife Mumtaz Mahal. Legend says that she made him promise to build her a mausoleum more beautiful than any the world had ever seen.

Arabesque is an art form originally from Asia Minor. It was later adapted by Muslim artisans into a highly formalised form of intertwined flowers and plants.

The Qur'aan, the Muslim holy book, was revealed to the Prophet Muhammad (pbuh) by the Angel Gabriel. Its verses are often inscribed in beautiful patterns by calligraphers.

First published in 2005 by Mantra Lingua Ltd.
Global House, 303 Ballards Lane, London N12 8NP
www.mantralingua.com

A CIP record for this book is available from the British Library